1719

THE TRAVELLER

THE TRAVELLER

by

WALTER DE LA MARE

with drawings by
John Piper

Faber and Faber Limited
24 Russell Square
London

First published in Mcmxlvi
by Faber and Faber Limited
24 Russell Square London W.C. 1
Second impression June Mcmxlvii
Printed in Great Britain by
R. MacLehose and Company Limited
The University Press Glasgow

821

1118

The four drawings by John Piper
lithographed at the Baynard Press
are to face pages 8, 12, 20, 30

THE TRAVELLER

' "I saw that the universe is not composed of dead matter
but is . . . a living presence." '

'Le soir vient; et le globe à son tour s'éblouit,
　　Devient un oeil énorme et regarde la nuit . . .

'Not in lone splendour hung aloft the night
　　But watching . . .'

This Traveller broke at length, toward set of sun,
Out from the gloom of towering forest trees;
Gasped, and drew rein: to gaze, in wonder, down
A bow-shaped gulf of shelving precipices.

The blue of space dreamed level with his eye.
A league beneath, like lava long at rest,
Lay a vast plateau, smooth as porphyry,
Its huge curve gradual as a woman's breast.

7

In saline marshes Titicaca lies—
Its ruins fabulous ere the Incas reigned:
Was this the like? A mountain sea? His eyes
Watched like a lynx. It still as death remained.

Not the least ripple broke the saffron sheen
Shed by the evening on this wild abyss.
Far countries he had roved, and marvels seen,
But never such a prodigy as this.

No. Water never in a monstrous mass
Rose to a summit like a rounded stone,
Ridged with concentric shadows. No morass
Were vast as this, or coloured zone by zone.

Vague relics haunted him of mythic tales,
Printed in books, or told him in his youth—
Deserts accursed; 'witched islands; sunken bells;
Fissures in space. . . Might one yet prove the truth?

Or, in his own sole being long confined,
Had he been lured into those outskirts where
A secret self is regent; and the mind
Reveals an actual none else can share?—

Prospects enchanting, dread, whereof as yet
No chart has record shown, could bearings tell;
Such as some fabulous Afreet might beget:
Clear as mirage, ev'n less attainable?

Stealthy in onset, between wake and sleep,
Such scenes, more moving than the earth can show,
May, self-created, in mutation sweep,
Silent and fugitive as April snow.

Or had he now attained the true intent
Of his unbroken pilgrimage? The sum
Of all his communings; and what they meant?
Was life at length to its Elysium come?

So flows experience: the vast Without;
Its microcosm, of the Soul, within;
Whereof the day-distracted eye may doubt,
But doubts no more as soon as dreams begin.

Thus mused this Traveller. Was he man or ghost?
Deranged by solitude? Or rapt away
To some unpeopled limbo of the lost—
Feint that the light of morning would betray?...

At verge of this huge void he camped for days;
Months of slow journeying from the haunts of men;
Till awe of it no longer could amaze,
And passion for venturing urged him on again.

Down, down into the abysm his mare, on hooves
Nimble as mountain-bred gazelle's, pricked on
From steep to steep, until through bouldered grooves
And shallowing streams she trod, their safety won—

An Arab lean and sleek, her surf-like mane
Tossed on a shoulder as of ivory made;
Full in the moonrise she approached the plain,
Was, with her master, in its beams arrayed.

He had scanned that lunar landscape when of old,
Tranced at a window as a child he had sat—
The Face, the Thorns, those craters grisly cold,
Volcanic seas now parched and desolate;

While from afar the bird of night bewailed
Her cruel ravishment. Even then he had pined,
Ere hope abandoned him, or courage failed,
To seek adventure, safety left behind.

Chilled by his travel in the shrewd clear air,
With wind-strown kindling-wood he built a fire;
Scant pasturage for man or beast was there,
And dreams but transiently assuage desire.

His supper done, he crouched beside the blaze,
Sharp-cheeked, wide-browed, and lost in reverie;
Flamelight and moonshine playing on his face,
The crackle of logs his only company.

When the dark tent of night at daybreak wanned,
He rose, remounted, and surveyed the vast
Convex of bloodshot stone that swept beyond
In arc enormous to the skies at last.

Great mountains he had ranged that lift their snow
In peaks sublime, which age to age remain
Unstirred by foot or voice; but here, a slow
Furtive foreboding crept into his brain

Of what yet lay before him—this Unknown;
In subtle feature so unlike the past
Havens of exile he had made his own,
Been restive in, or wearied of at last.

Soon as the risen sun rilled down its heat,
A dewy mist, in this huge hollow pent,
Washed like a sea of milk his Arab's feet.
And rainbows arched before him as he went.

The call of waters kept his ears a-cock—
Creeks fed by cataracts now left behind.
Forests of fungi in the lichened rock
Showed ashen wan and grey as withy-wind;

Spawn of a gendering hour, yet hoar with age,
They stood sun-bleached, ephemera of the night,
And—thing past even speculation strange—
Growths never grazed till now by human sight.

What tinier atomies of life were bred
Beneath their skin-thin gills, tents, muted bells,
Eye could not guess—as procreant a bed
As is man's body with its countless cells.

The furtive mist, these clustered funguses—
Minutest stirrings of primeval slime,
The empty heavens, aloof and measureless,
Illusions seemed, not only of space, but time.

From microscopical to the immense—
Mere magnitude of little moment is;
But violent contrast shakes man's confidence
Even in what lies plain before his eyes.

Birds of rare flight and hue, of breed unknown,
Rose, wheeled, fled onward, mewling as they went—
And left him—more forsaken and alone;
Sun for sole guidance in his slow ascent.

But borne not far upon the windless air,
The fickle fleet-winged creatures turned anon;
Came stooping backward on his face to stare:
Broke out in cries again; again, were gone:

Curious, but fearless of what never yet
Had on these mighty slopes been seen to appear;
With soft-tongued jargoning they his way beset,
Sadder than love-lorn pewit's on the ear.

Nor was it only stone that made reply.
Their sweetness echoed in his heart. Delight
And love long pent in fadeless memory
Welled to his eyes. He watched them out of sight.

What meaning harbours in a bird's lone note
Secret as music is; ineffable:
With Song of the Sirens it has been forgot:
But long he journeyed on beneath its spell.

Westward to eastward, wide as gaze could scan,
Shallowly troughed, the void savanna swept:
The dead of all the armies doomed by Man
Might, biding ransom, in its folds have slept.

And, hollow as sinister beating of a drum
The rock resounded when, with sudden bound,
His beast beneath him, on the treacherous scum,
Slipped, and, with snort of fear, her balance found.

That night, while yet in darkness lapped, it seemed
He had leapt from sleep, that instant made aware
The rock beneath had trembled while he dreamed,
Bleached of a sudden by the lightning's glare.

Foreboding perils unconceived before,
He woke when dawn again suffused the sky.
His earth, once stable, now proved insecure:
He sat and watched it with unwinking eye;

While chattering voices wrangled in his head:
"Alas, what horror of the soul is this?"
"Beware! Away!" "Far better thou were dead
Than face the ordeal that now before thee lies!"

A plaintive whinny in the early air,
For company calling, solace brought. He smiled.
And in sweet converse with his timorous mare
Soothed her disquiet, and his own beguiled.

Towards noon an arid wind from out the East
Waxed, waned; and failed as they approached—these two,
In close companionship of man and beast,
To where the plain they paced lapsed into blue.

His aching eyes rejoiced. No more there showed
Branched veins of sanguine in a milk-pale stone;
An ever deepening azure gloomed and glowed
In shine and shadow as they journeyed on:

Turquoise, and sapphire, speedwell, columbine.
When clouds minute, like scales of fish, are seen
Dappling an April daybreak, then, divine
As Eros' eyes, there shows a blue between,

Tranquil, wan, infinite. So, pale to dark,
A dark as dazzling as the tropic deep,
Loomed now the prospect toward his distant mark,
When yet again he laid him down to sleep.

In this oblivion he dreamed a dream:—
He dreamed the transitory host of men,
Debased by pride, lust, greed and self-esteem,
Had gone their way; that Earth was freed again.

Their minds had brewed a poison in the blood;
The sap of their own nature had decayed.
They had chosen evil, had resigned the good;
False, faithless, pitiless, and of nought afraid.

Nature, released from this vile incubus,
Had wooed into being creatures of other kind,
Resembling those long since deemed fabulous,
As exquisite in aspect as in mind.

Beings, too, once adored for beauty and grace,
Who had left but echoes in the mirroring air,
Had sought again their bygone dwelling-place;
As happy birds in springtime homeward fare.

And he?—the sport of contraries in sleep!—
To childhood had returned; gone grief and woe;
That Eden of the heart, and fellowship
With innocence, that only children know;

And in a garden played, serene, alone;
Bird, flower, water, shining in his eyes;
And magic hidd'n in even the tiniest stone . . .
When, suddenly, a Trumpet rent the skies:

To Judgement had been called the Sons of Light,
The stellar host, the Sun and all his brood:
Rank beyond rank, height above heavenly height,
Within the eternal peace of God they stood,

Hymning his glory. And, alas, he knew
That, chosen envoy of the Earth, he had come,
Garbed in her beauty, and enraptured too;
But, though he had yearned for joy, his soul was dumb.

And by unuttered edict exiled thence,
He had fallen, as Satan fell, in leaden dismay,
And thus had wakened to the rock-land whence
His spirit, in fantasy, had winged away. . .

On high a dwindling, sun-bedazzled moon
Paled in the homeless solitudes of space,
Casting gaunt shadow here—his vision gone—
For void companionship in this bitter place.

He, Envoy of the Earth!—that mothering breast;
Those Suns and Sons, what meaning could he find?—
A cold satanic irony at best,
Or scoff of that mocking-bird in sleep, his mind.

Oh, that he had but one bright candle here
To pierce the double-dark of body and soul!
Could but a strain of music reach his ear
To ease this heartsick wretchedness and dole!

From lifted brow his leaden-lidded eyes
Searched the vast furrows of unanswering stone
To where the cedar-arc'd abyss must rise
Whence he had journeyed to this end, alone.

Gazing, he mused, beset by mystery,
Mere Sentience in the silence of the night;
Could Earth itself a living creature be,
And he its transitory parasite?—

A frosted incubus, by the cold congealed,
Doubting his senses, vacantly aware
Of what already instinct had revealed—
His deadliest danger now was blank despair.

Like an old zany, he seemed, who, year by year,
The slave has been of an Excelsior,
Its goal Eureka; and when that draws near
Hears fleshless knuckles on his chamber-door!

Or like a doting lover who at last
By one whose source had seemed of heavenly grace
Forsaken is, in outer darkness cast,
Her cheating blandishment a Lamia's face.

Meagre his saddlebag as camel's hump
When, sand-marooned, she staggers to her doom.
As shrunken too, his Arab's ribs and rump
Showed taut as vellum stretched upon a drum.

He strove in vain to reason, numbed with sleep,
But conscious that at first faint token of dawn,
Wraiths at whose beauty even the blind might weep,
Wooed to his solitude, had come, and gone—

Wraiths all but lost to memory, whose love
Had burned in hearts that never more would beat;
Of whose compassion sense could bring no proof,
Though solace 'twas beyond all telling sweet—

Like flowers that a child brings home; to fade.
Alas, alas, no longing could restore
Life to the faithful by neglect betrayed!
Too late for ransom; they'd return no more—

Had left him, like a castaway adrift,
Lashed to a raft upon a chartless sea,
His only motion the huge roller's lift,
Its depths his only hope at peace to be.

"Sea"! when this waste of stone in which he lay
Like night-blue porcelain was, untinged with red.
But when his cracked lips stirred, as if to pray,
He caught but leaf-dry whisper of what they said.

So tense was this his solitude—the sky
Its mute and viewless canopy—that when
His grieved 'O God!' was followed by a sigh,
It seemed eternity had breathed amen.

Ay, as if cock, horizon-far, had crowed,
His heart, like Peter's, had been rent in twain.
At pang of it his grief again up-flowed,
Though its "Who's there?" called only in his brain. . .

On, and still on he pressed—scorched heel to nape,
Hunched in his saddle from the noonday's glare—
Watched by a winged thing, high in heaven, agape
To ken aught stirring in a tract so bare,

Which leaf or blade of grass could never yield.
A vitreous region, like a sea asleep,
Crystalline, convex, tideless and congealed,
Profounder far than Tuscarora Deep,

Further than sight could reach, before him lay.
Head bent, eyes fixed—drowsed by recurrent stroke
Of tic-tac ice-like hoof-beats, wits astray,
He slipped again from real to dream: awoke

To find himself marooned beneath a dome
Of star-pricked vacancy, and darkness near;
His breast bespattered with his Arab's foam,
And—trotting at his heels—the spectre, Fear:

Whose fell pursuit, unhastening, pace for pace—
Like Lama of Tibet in waking trance—
His very soul for quarry in the chase,
Forbade all hazard of deliverance:

A shapeless shape of horror, mildew-blue,
With naked feet, blank eyes, and leprous face,
Insane with lust, that ever nearer drew,
Tarrying for midnight and the dread embrace.

Foes of the soul there are, corrupt, malign,
Taint of whose malice is so evil a blight
That ev'n the valiant must hope resign
Unless God's mercy give them means for flight.

Witless as wild bird tangled in a net,
He dared not turn his head, but galloped on,
Spurs red at heel, his body drenched with sweat,
Until, with nerve renewed, but strength nigh gone,

He slowed his pace to listen; gasped, fordone;
Drew rein, dismounted. . . But, the peril past,
His cheek was fallen in like that of one
Whom mortal stroke of fate has felled at last;

And in a moment aged him many years—
Edict beyond the mind to comprehend.
Plaiting cramped fingers in the elf-locked mane,
'Come, now,' he muttered, 'we must rest, my friend.'

The creature's sunken eyeballs, scurfed with rheum
And mute with misery, returned his gaze;
And thus they communed in the gathering gloom,
Nought but the love between them left to graze.

She pawed the unnatural ice, tossed her small head,
By inarticulate alarm distressed;
Baring her teeth, squealed faintly, smitten with dread;
And, snuggling closer, lipped her master's breast.

His breath rasped harshly—wind in blasted wheat;
Through fret of her coarse mane his sun-parched eyes,
Their swol'n lids blackened by the daylong heat,
Swept the dim vacuum of earth and skies.

'Quiet, dear heart! The end is nearing now.
Into disaster thou hast been betrayed.'
He smoothed her gentle muzzle, kissed her brow.
'Nought worse than one more night to live,' he said.

'We both are mortal, both have fallen at last
Into disgrace. But had I swerved aside,
And safety found, what peace, the danger past,
Is his who sleeps with Terror for his bride?

But one night more. And then must come what may.
But never mistress held man's life in fee
As mine has been. And how could speech convey
The woe, forlorn one, that I feel for thee!'

So grieved he in his heart. This comrade dear!
His gentle hand upon her shoulder lay
Though still she shivered, twitching flank and ear,
In this drear wilderness so far astray.

Long stood he motionless, while overhead
The circling constellations, east to west,
Misting the infinite, their effluence shed—
Friends long familiar on how many a quest!

From this dark timeless absence of the mind
It seemed an inward voice had summoned him:—
'See! See!'—a whisper fainter than the wind
Or ripple of water lipped on Lethe's brim.

24

For now—the zenith darkening—opal-pale,
As if the earth its secret well-spring were—
Softly as flowers of night their scents exhale—
A strange and deepening lustre tinged the air,

Gentle and radiant. So, from off the sea
May mirrored moonbeams, when calm waters lave
A rock-bound coast, steal inward silently,
Blanching the sombre vaultings of a cave.

Not rock his roof-tree here, but hollow sky;
Not reflex moon-ray, but a phantom light,
Like hovering, pervasive reverie
Of Mind supreme, illumining the night.

Rapt in this loveliness, his spellbound face,
To travail the while, and famine, reconciled,
Of fret and weariness shed every trace,
As sleep brings comfort to a tired-out child:

Sleep to a body so pure and exquisite
Like manna it is, at gilding sunrise seen;
The senses so untrammelled that as yet
No more than frailest barrier lies between

Soul and reality. Thus beauty may
Pierce through the mists that worldly commerce brings,
Imagination's blindness wash away,
And—bird at daybreak—lend the spirit wings.

Even the little ant, devoid of fear,
Prowling beneath the shadow of a man,
Conscious may be of occult puissance near,
Whose origin it neither recks, nor can.

So, though he too was now but vaguely aware
Whence welled this boon of benison and peace,
In awe of a mystery so divinely fair,
Tears gushed within him, not of grief but bliss.

Courage revived, like greenness after rain.
Slowly he turned; looked back. And in amaze—
A waif self-exiled from the world of men—
Trembled at sight of what now met his gaze:—

The hushed and visionary host of those
Who, like himself, had faced life's long duress,
Its pangs and horrors, anguish, hardship, woes,
Their one incentive ever on to press,

Defying dread and danger—and in vain:
Not to achieve a merely temporal goal,
Not for bright glory, praise, or greed of gain,
But in that secret craving of the soul

For what no name has; flower of hidden stem:—
The unreturned of kindless land and sea;
Venturers, voyagers, dreamers, seers—ay, them
The Angel of Failure hails with rhapsody.

Him, too, for some rare destiny designed,
Who, in faith and love, has ranged; unmarked, alone;
Though means to share it he will never find
Since its sole language is unique—his own:

Great deeds win sweet renown: the hope forlorn
May perish, and none know what fate it braved;
The self content, at ease, has yet forsworn
The scope that still awaits the soul that's saved:

Faith in a love that can no respite have,
Being its sole resource and anodyne—
Impassioned love, its goal beyond the grave,
However short it fall of the divine.

Ay, even though Man have but one earthly life,
Cradle to grave, wherein to joy and grieve?
His grace were yet the agony and strife
In quest of what no mortal can achieve.

'Angel', forsooth! Bleak visage, frigid breast,
Passionless Nemesis, the heart for prey,
She goads her votary with insane unrest
And smiles upon him when she stoops to slay!

Strange beauty theirs, this host—in rapt array,
Spectral and motionless, intent, and dumb,
Laved in light's loveliness they stretched away
Homage ironic to his Kingdom Come!

Less a mere castaway of flesh and bone,
Defenceless, lost, whom Fate will overwhelm,
He now appeared, than—child of genius—one
Who explores pure fantasy's unbounded realm;

And being at length confronted by ordeal
No human consciousness could comprehend,
A preternatural ecstacy can feel—
Life's kiss of rapture at life's journey's end.

'All hail!' he muttered; paused; then laid him low,
His crazed head pillowed on his Arab's flank;
Prostrate with thirst and weariness and woe,
Into a plumbless deep of sleep he sank.

What visitants of earth or air drew near
Rider and horse in these stark hours of night—
Sylphs of the wilderness or demon drear,
Gazed long and softly, and again took flight,

No sense ajar revealed; nor echo of
Music ethereal, pining sweet and shrill
Of voices in the vaults of heaven above,
The angelic solitudes of Israfel . . .

When daybreak moved above the hushed expanse,
By ague shaken, he awoke. Aware
Nought now could shield him from life's last mischance,
With tranquil mind he breathed the scentless air.

This sterile world!—no weed here raised its head;
No bird on dew-plashed wing, his ear to bless,
Flew up to greet the dayspring; but instead,
A tense unfathomable silentness

Engulfed the enormous convex, stony-still,
Of hueless, lucent crystal where he lay,
Shivering in fever in the sunless chill,
Its centre now scarce half a league away.

He rose; the rustle of his raiment seemed
A desecration of the quietude
Brimming its vacancy; as if there dreamed
A presence here where none had dared intrude

Since waters from waters had divided been,
World from the heavens, the land from ocean freed;
And fruitful trees sprang up, with leafage green,
And earth put forth the herb that yieldeth seed.

'Come, now', he whispered softly; paused; aghast,
Deeming his faithful one had found reprieve;
Had fled away, all tribulation past,
Where even the soul-less languish not nor grieve;

But green-grey willows hang their tresses down;
The heron fishes in his plashy pool;
There, in her beauty floats the silent swan—
Shady and verdurous and calm and cool:

Meadows where asphodel and cowslips blow,
And sunlit summer clouds dissolve in rain—
Her earthly paradise! At length! But no;
The gentle creature heard, had stirred again.

Scrabbling her fore-hoofs on the treacherous waste,
She rose, stood trembling; with sepulchral sigh
Turned her night-blinded eyes, her master faced;
And patiently, piteously set out to die.

To eyried bird above, now rosed with light,
Of insectine dimensions they appeared;
Like emmet creeping, or the weevil-mite
That in a mouldering ship at sea is reared.

Sable in plumage, ruff, and naked head,
Superb in flight, and poised upon his shelf
Of viewless air, he tarried for the dead,
And watched, indifferent as Death himself.

Though the great globe around them grudged them tomb,
Feast they would be for both these ravening foes—
Horseman and Arab, who had dared to roam
Beneath these mountains' never-melting snows.

Halt, maimed and impotent, still travelling on,
O'er very Eye of Earth they made their way,
Till rimmed into the east the risen sun
Flooding its orbit with the joy of day—

That Eye of Heaven, mansion of secret light,
Whose beams of all that's lovely are the shrine,
Procreant, puissant, arbiter of Sight,
Emblem and symbol of the light divine—

So brilliant the least flaw beneath their feet
A tiny shadow cast where nought there was
Taller than locust in the rilling heat
To check the splendour of this sea of glass.

And if pure radiance could pure music be,
And quiet supreme its tabernacle were,
This orb, now blazing in its majesty,
With a sublime Hosanna rent the air.

Moved by an impulse beyond wit to scan,
His poor rags stirring in a fitful breeze,
This worn, outwearied, errant son of man
Paused, bowed his head, fell down upon his knees;

And, with a faint and lamentable cry,
Poured hoarsely forth a babble of praise and prayer,
Sun on his brows, above the boundless sky,
No living soul to hear or heed him there . . .

A self there is that listens in the heart
To what is past the range of human speech,
Which yet has urgent tidings to impart—
The all-but-uttered, and yet out of reach.

Beneath him an immeasurable well
Of lustrous crystal motionlessly black
Deeped on. And as he gazed—marvel past words to tell—
It seemed to him a presence there gazed back:

Rapt, immaterial, remote; ev'n less
In substance than is image of the mind;
And yet, in all-embracing consciousness
Of its own inmost being; elsewise blind:

Past human understanding to conceive;
Of virgin innocence, yet source of all
That matter had the power to achieve
Ere Man created was, ere Adam's fall:

And in its midst a mote scarce visible—
Himself: the momentary looking-glass
Of Nature, which a moment may annul,
And with earth's hosts may into nothing pass:

The flux of change. Ay, this poor Traveller too—
Soon to be dust, though once erect, elate,
From whose clear gaze a flame divine burned through;
A son of God—no sport of Time or Fate:

It seemed his heart was broken; his whole life long
Concentred in this moment of desire;
Its woe, its rapture, transient as the song
The Phoenix sings upon her funeral pyre.

'Alas', he gasped—his journey now at end;
Breathed softly out his last of many sighs;
Flung forth his hands, and motionless remained,
Drenched through with day; and darkness in his eyes . . .

Head drooped, knees sagging, his forsaken jade—
Her stark hide gilded by the eastern sun,
Her abject carcass in its glory arrayed—
As though in fear to break his prayers, drowsed on.

But, as an acid frets its way through steel,
Into her sentience at length there crept
A deeper hush no silence could conceal—
And Death for long has never secret kept,

Though shadow-close it mime its sister, Sleep.
The creature nearer drew—reluctant, slow,
As if, like motherless child, to sigh and weep,
Too young the import of its loss to know.

Ears pricked, reins dangling, thus a while she stayed—
Of that in watch above full well aware:
'See, now, dear master, here I wait!'   She neighed,
And stooping, snuffed the rags, the matted hair;

Then, of a sudden, in panic dread, upreared,
Plunged, wheeled, drew back, her eyeballs gleaming white,
And urged to frenzy by the thing she feared
From all that love had left on earth took flight . . .

Sweet is that Earth, though sorrow and woe it have,
Though parched, at length, the milk within its breast;
And then the night-tide of the all-welcoming grave
For those who weary, and a respite crave:
Inn at the cross roads, and the traveller's rest . . .